EVEN WHEN IT'S RAINING CATS AND DOGS, YOU'VE JUST GOTTA MAKE THE SUN SHINE WITHIN YOU.

THIS SUNNY LITTLE BOOK BELONGS TO ...

A BOOK OF

SUNSHINE

FEATURING TINY MIRACLES, MOVING CLOUDS AND SUNBURSTS

A BOOK OF
SUNSHINE

FEATURING TINY MIRACLES, MOVING CLOUDS AND SUNBURSTS

BILL ZIMMERMAN & PATRICIA KITCHEN

ILLUSTRATIONS BY TOM BLOOM

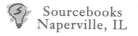

Sourcebooks
Naperville, IL

Published by Sourcebooks
P.O. Box 372
Naperville, IL   60566
(630) 961-3900
FAX: 630-961-2168

ISBN 1-57071-159-3

For my Cousins Ruth and Judy, and Aunt Ann and Uncle George, who have brought sunshine into my own life. With thanks.

—BZ

To my two grandmothers, Ida, whom I knew and loved, and Kate, whom I never met.

—PK

To My WIFE, THE UNIVERSE;
To My DAUGHTER, THE MOON AND THE STARS;
AND TO My SON, OF COURSE, THE SUN.

TB

Suntroduction

Of course, if we had the power, we would have had a ray of sunshine beam at you when you first opened this book...but that was somewhat beyond our technical ability.

If we could, we would have had a handful of confetti pop out at you when you opened this book's first page...but some of you might not have liked the mess.

You see, we wanted to present you with a book of cheer, and when we came down to it, we decided the best way we knew to bring light into your life was through our simple words and drawings. Maybe they'll encourage you to think some new thoughts to replace the tired, gloomy old ones you'd like to escape; maybe, they'll even make you smile and chuckle.

For we well know that when your lips part into a smile, and your eyes crinkle with laughter, your face becomes beautiful and glowing...like the sun.

If the truth be told, only you have the power to bring sunshine into your life and move those foreboding clouds. Believe us, it's not so hard to do. All you have to do is give yourself a break and say the forgiving words which will allow you to become sunny and find the life-giving light glowing within you. Our words and drawings are just to get you started.

We mean it when we say the only way to move the clouds in your life is. . . THINK SUNSHINE.

Yours sincerely,

Bill Zimmerman

Patricia Kitchen

and

Tom Bloom

P.S. Throughout this book you'll find pages of "Tiny Miracles." These are the simple, wonderful things we sometimes take for granted, but which make up the great miracle of our own lives. Space is provided for you to write your own "tiny miracles." You'll find pages, too, to write, color or drawn your own bright sunspots. There are even some Solargrams you can fill in and sent to that special someone.

So, enjoy!

MORNING

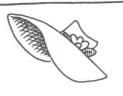

S U N

TINY MIRACLES

A FRESH CUP OF YOUR FAVORITE BREW

SOMEONE WHO'S IN LOVE WITH YOU

WALKING BY THE SEA

FEELING A SENSE OF COMMUNITY

WRITE — AND RECORD — YOUR OWN — TINY MIRACLES — HERE

When you wake up
in the morning, say "YES"
a hundred times. Get up on
your toes, now pirouette as
you look into a mirror, and
laugh at yourself.

S U N

TINY MIRACLES

A NEIGHBORLY CHAT WITH ONE YOU DON'T KNOW

FIRST FOOTPRINTS IN A FRESH FIELD OF SNOW

A BIRD'S JOYOUS MORNING SONG

HELPING EVERYONE GET ALONG

WRITE AND RECORD YOUR OWN TINY MIRACLES HERE

Listen to the song
the sun's beams sing as
they dance across your face,

MOVING CLOUDS

Don't Let a Little Cloud Spoil Your Day.

Make Today Your Special Day.

Negative thoughts are
like thieves who steal your
energy and leave you powerless.
Fill your head instead
with pictures of your greatest
successes. Each of us has some.

S
U
N

SUNDRIES

OPEN UP YOUR PETALS. ON SUNDAY, PIN BLOSSOMS ALL OVER YOUR CLOTHES. IMAGINE YOU ARE A NEW SPECIES OF FLORA, HOW SHALL YOU BE IDENTIFIED?

B
U
R
S
T

LET SOMEONE ELSE'S MAGIC WORK ON YOU.

Be like a baby for a
little while. You haven't
any regrets and your future
is simply grand. Promise
yourself (cross your heart)
that you will try hard
in the days ahead to
reap that glowing
future.

RAINY DAY PAGE

IF YOU'RE
LUCKY, YOU'LL
DISCOVER A
RAINBOW
AFTER THE STORM.

IF YOU'RE
WISE, YOU'LL
SAVE THAT

RAINBOW
FOR THE NEXT
RAINY DAY.

 ORDER SOME EGGS SUNNYSIDE UP.

In the shower, imagine yourself finally under those magical waterfalls in Hawaii or Jamaica.

SUN

TINY MIRACLES

OPENING A NEW BOX OF CRAYONS

FINDING SOCKS THAT DON'T STAY ON

GETTING BETTER AFTER A COLD

FEELING YOUNG AS YOU GROW OLD

WRITE AND RECORD YOUR OWN TINY MIRACLES HERE

Drape a sheet around yourself, put on some old sandals, for today, you are Zeus. At whom will you hurl your thunderbolt?
Or, are you Athena? With whom will you share your wisdom?

MOVING CLOUDS

MAKE A CLEAN SWEEP OF THINGS.

UNPLUG YOUR CLOCK FOR A DAY.

Hug your dog or cat a lot. You'll see how their love and warmth will calm and comfort you.

◧ ▯ SUN SPOTS ⟫

≫ A SAFE HAVEN WHERE YOU CAN WRITE SOMETHING BRIGHT ≪

READ THE FUNNY PAPERS.

Think of all the wonderful things you would miss if you weren't here to enjoy them. Remember the beach and the ocean, the wind blowing on your face, the beautiful seashells, the fresh smell of the saltair.

TINY MIRACLES

GREEN BANANAS TURNING YELLOW

THE JOY IT BRINGS TO SAY HELLO

YOUR CHRISTMAS ORNAMENT FROM FIRST GRADE

A GIVEN GIFT THAT IS HAND·MADE

WRITE  AND RECORD  YOUR OWN  TINY MIRACLES HERE

MOVING CLOUDS

WE MUST EACH OF US DO OUR SHARE.

BREATHE DEEPLY. BREATHE SLOWLY.

As you hear or read them, write down quotations that inspire you. When you feel low, thumb through your collection and pull out the quotes that cheer you up. Hey, imagine you are Confucious and make up some sayings of your own. (Bet you're much wiser than you thought you were.)

S
U
N

SUNDRIES

TAKE YOURSELF OUT TO AFTERNOON TEA. LISTEN AS THE MUSIC WAFTS THROUGH THE ROOM. TRY ONE OF THOSE LITTLE SANDWICHES, STEEP IN THE TRADITION.

B
U
R
S
T

TICKLE SOMEONE YOU LOVE.

TINY MIRACLES

CHUCKLES, GIGGLES, GUFFAWS AND LAUGHTER

FINALLY GETTING WHAT YOU'RE AFTER

A BUTTERFLY THAT'S LANDED ON YOUR HAND

ADMIRING, NOT COUNTING, EVERY GRAIN OF SAND

WRITE AND RECORD YOUR OWN TINY MIRACLES HERE

MOVING CLOUDS

LOOK AHEAD FOR THE SHAPE OF THINGS TO COME.

 DISREGARD THE RAIN.

Go to the kitchen and
smell the herbs and spices.
Be comforted by their aroma.

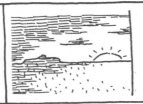

SUN

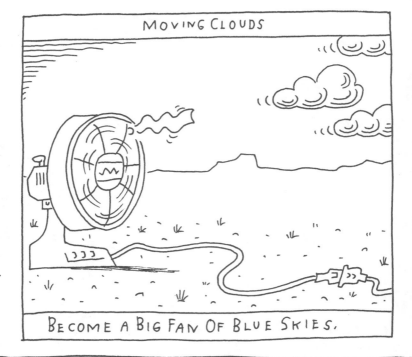

MOVING CLOUDS

BECOME A BIG FAN OF BLUE SKIES.

BURST

PART YOUR HAIR ON THE OTHER SIDE.

Imagine that you are the scientist creating a new gene for laughter and joy. And you're willing to be the first test case.

TINY MIRACLES

A BABY'S GRASPING FINGERS

A LOVER'S KISS THAT LINGERS

A SPARKLE IN SOMEONE'S SMILING EYES

THE SOUL REVEALED BY QUIET SIGHS

WRITE AND RECORD YOUR OWN TINY MIRACLES HERE

Grab a magic marker and a piece of colored paper. Write down #1 and pin it to your shirt. Wear it proudly all day.

» A Safe Haven Where You Can Draw Something Bright «

Sun Spots

JUMP FOR JOY.

When you suddenly catch sight of your reflection in a store window, smile at it... it will smile back. Don't make any quick judgments about the person you see.

RAINY DAY PAGE

A PUDDLE IS MUCH MORE THAN A REMNANT OF A RAINY MORNING.

IN THE SPACE OF A SPLASH IT IS THE PASSAGEWAY BACK TO YOUR CHILDHOOD.

B
U
R
S
T

MAKE YOUR FRIENDS LAUGH FIRST.

MOVING CLOUDS

TRIM YOUR TROUBLES TO A MANAGEABLE SIZE.

HUG SOMEONE OVER THE TELEPHONE.

Imagine for a moment that you could taste a slice of a rainbow or even hold it in your hands. Doesn't that make you feel a lot better? It looks as if it tastes like sherbet. Does it?

SUNDRIES

ON A CRISP WINTER NIGHT, PLANT A GARDEN IN YOUR MIND. MAP OUT WHERE YOU'LL WANT EACH FLOWER TO BE. SOON IT WILL BE SPRING,

WALK ALONG THE OCEAN'S EDGE.

TINY MIRACLES

YOUR BEST FRIEND'S ARRIVAL

AN INSTINCT FOR SURVIVAL

TO BE TREATED LIKE A GUEST

YOU, AT YOUR VERY BEST

 WRITE  AND RECORD YOUR OWN TINY MIRACLES  HERE

My dear Friend,

If I could pluck a star from the night sky, I'd give it to you to brighten your day.

Devotedly,

SUN-LARGRAM

To

MOVING CLOUDS

DON'T BE AFRAID TO ASK FOR HELP.

TURN YOUR IMAGINATION LOOSE.

Be brave for yourself.
Read aloud a beautiful poem
or psalm. Try to commit it to
memory so you can call upon it
when you need some cheer.

TINY MIRACLES

A SUMMER'S
B U Z Z I N G
BUMBLE
BEE

HELPING SOMEONE
OUT
QUITE
HUMBLY

THE SMELL OF GRASS
THAT'S
FRESHLY   MOWN

PHOTOS OF LOVED ONES
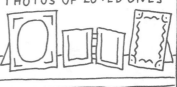
LONG SINCE GROWN

WRITE · AND RECORD · YOUR OWN · TINY MIRACLES · HERE

Cultivate a butterfly garden,
Make friends with a caterpillar,

SUN

SUNDRIES

GO TO THE ZOO. VISIT THE MONKEYS. WATCH THEM ROMP AND PLAY. THEY ARE NOISY AND FUNNY. DO YOU SEE ANY OF YOURSELF IN THEM? THEN DO A LITTLE MONKEY DANCE. GO AHEAD, WE DARE YOU.

BURST

DRAW A WISH USING ALL THE COLORS.

Look through your baby pictures and then remember all the troubles you have overcome since those photos were taken. You are stronger than you think,

S U N

RAINY DAY PAGE

GREET A DARK AND STORMY DAY AS AN INVITATION TO STAY COZY INDOORS, SEEK OUT THOSE LITTLE TREASURES THAT YOU OFTEN TAKE FOR GRANTED.

B U R S T

MEMORIZE A POEM. RECITE IT.

Look beyond yourself and help someone. Come out of your shell. Please.

SUN

SUN SPOTS

>> A SAFE HAVEN WHERE YOU CAN DOODLE SOMETHING BRIGHT <<

BURST

PLACE A SEA SHELL TO YOUR EAR.

Reconnect with the world. Call up an old friend you've lost touch with. Don't think of reasons not to. Just dial the number. Now.

S U N

TINY MIRACLES

THE FRESHNESS OF A SPRINGTIME RAIN

EASING SOMEONE ELSE'S PAIN

DOING YOUR BEST

THOUGH IT MAY BE HARD

THE MANY WORLDS

OFFERED BY A LIBRARY CARD

WRITE AND RECORD YOUR OWN TINY MIRACLES HERE

Sit down in a wonderful spot at the museum, and lose yourself in the grandeur of this great palace. How can you be sad when you're enveloped by such beauty?

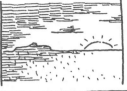

MOVING CLOUDS

MAKING MISTAKES IS REALLY A WAY OF LEARNING.

PLAY THE KAZOO,

Think of yourself as a clown cheering up sick children; then think of yourself as that same child laughing.

TINY MIRACLES

A PILLOW THAT SMELLS LIKE PINE

SAYING A PRAYER

RECEIVING A SIGN

A LITTLE SALTY TEAR OF JOY

A BABY GIRL OR A BABY BOY

 WRITE AND RECORD YOUR OWN TINY MIRACLES HERE

Eat lunch today with someone you haven't seen for a while. Tell them your favorite joke.

RAINY DAY PAGE

A SUN SHOWER IS LIKE A TEACHER.

IT CHANGES THE WAY YOU THINK AND POINTS OUT LIFE'S WONDERFUL CONTRADICTIONS.

MAKE A SUNBEAM PIE. SERVE IT TO A FRIEND.

Bring back from your walks a pebble, a shell, a twig or a pinecone to look at and touch from time to time. It will remind you of a golden moment.

SUNDRIES

WHEN YOU FEEL HEAVY AND EARTHBOUND, FIND A FIELD AND GO FLY A KITE. WHY SHOULDN'T YOUR HEART AND SPIRITS SOAR, AS WELL?

BURST

SEND YOURSELF A LOVE LETTER.

Shop in a Five & Dime. Stop in the children's department, and buy yourself a gift for under $2. Will it be soap bubbles, or chalk, or crayons?

MOVING CLOUDS

Nº 16 K
pg 8

MAKE SURE YOUR LIFE AND SOUL ARE ON THE SAME PATH.

PUT A RAINBOW IN YOUR POCKET.

Shake up your routine today. Eat something new for lunch. Walk a different route home so you'll see a diversity of sights. Switch radiostations. You're not really so stuck at all.

SUN

TINY MIRACLES

THE SERENITY OF A WATERFALL

A LONG LOST FRIEND THAT GIVES YOU A CALL

HAPPY MEMORIES THAT COME BACK TO YOU

RECOGNITION FOR THE WORK YOU DO

WRITE

AND RECORD

YOUR OWN

TINY MIRACLES

HERE

Stand in a place where you can see the entire sky with no buildings blocking the view. This will be your own panoramic movie screen. Let the changing clouds and passing birds entertain you in slow motion.

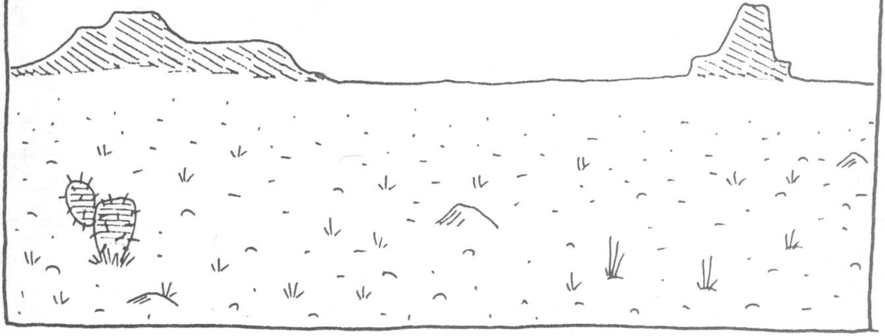

S U N

TINY MIRACLES

A JACK-IN-THE-BOX

CUCKOO CLOCKS

A SINGING FROG

A LOVING DOG

 WRITE 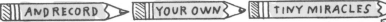 AND RECORD > YOUR OWN > TINY MIRACLES > HERE

Stop into a shop that sells body oils and lotions. Spend some time sniffing, spraying, and spreading the various samples. Reek. Smell. Be odoriferous. But enjoy every second of it.

SUN

RAINY DAY PAGE

WHEN TEARS RUN DOWN YOUR CHEEK, PUT THEM TO A GOOD USE. QUICKLY CATCH THEM AND WATER ANY SEEDLINGS THAT YOU HAVE PLANTED.

BURST

TAKE A NAP AFTER LUNCH.

Get yourself into a park. Take a walk. Borrow a dog, if you don't have one, to take you for a walk. Just get out of the house when the four walls threaten to drive you crazy.

SUN

MOVING CLOUDS

SOLVE YOUR PROBLEMS WITH WHAT'S AT HAND.

BURST

 BLOW SOME SOAP BUBBLES.

When you've got no one to hug, just pay a visit to the teddy bear corner of your local toy store. Try out all the bears until you find the best hugger. Bring that one home and hug it all night long.

SUNDRIES

MAKE A MASK USING SOMEONE ELSE'S FACE OR A DESIGN OF YOUR OWN DOING. HAVE A DAY OF MASQUERADE. IT MAY HELP YOU TO DISCOVER YOU.

TAKE A LONG, LONG WALK.

Buy a cheap fish tank and stock it with a few exotic fish. There are not too many things that compare with the beauty and serenity of watching fish swim back and forth in their lit tank.

SUN

MOVING CLOUDS

BE AWARE, EVEN WHEN THERE'S NOT A CLOUD IN THE SKY.

BURST

 DAYDREAM.

Love your body, Despite what advertisers say, the only perfect body is yours, that's because you're inside it, treat this body well, Hug it at leastonce a day,

SUN

TINY MIRACLES

THE SHOCK OF SPRING'S FORSYTHIA BUDS

THE SIMPLISTIC BEAUTY OF SOAP SUDS

CHOCOLATE·COVERED STRAWBERRIES

BELIEF IN SUCH THINGS AS FAERIES

WRITE AND RECORD YOUR OWN TINY MIRACLES HERE

SUN

SUN SPOTS

» A Safe Haven Where You Can Create Something Bright «

BURST

RECYCLE. PAPER, PLASTIC, IDEAS.

Ask your friends and family what they do to banish the blues. Try the ones that make sense to you.

S U N

MOVING CLOUDS

CLIMB ABOVE ALL THE CLAMOR. ENJOY THE VIEWS.

B U R S T

 FEED THE BIRDS AND SQUIRRELS.

Pretend you
are a Superhero
and your mission
is to go out and
rescue yourself,

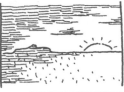

SUN

TINY MIRACLES

A CHILD'S HUG

A LADY BUG

A SUNNY DAY

A PLACE TO PLAY

WRITE AND RECORD YOUR OWN TINY MIRACLES HERE

CUT THIS OUT

FILL THIS IN

Greetings _____,

Wouldn't it be
great fun if we
could walk together
on a bridge of
rainbows.

Your friend,

S-LARGRAM

© 1997 · BILL ZIMMERMAN · PATRICIA KITCHEN · TOM BLOOM
"A BOOK OF SUNSHINE" SOURCEBOOKS INC. PUBLISHER

To

& Night

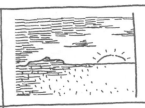

S U N

TINY MIRACLES

THE FIRST SIGNS OF SPRING

A LITTLE BELL'S

RING

TIME WITH A FRIEND

A SMILE YOU

CAN SEND

 WRITE AND RECORD YOUR OWN TINY MIRACLES HERE

Try to squeeze all of your
sorrow into a bottle
and toss it into
the ocean.

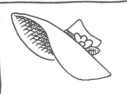

SUN

SUNDRIES

LISTEN TO THE RUSTLE OF AUTUMN LEAVES AS YOU WALK THROUGH THEM. ABSORB THEIR SMELL AS YOU TOSS THEM INTO THE AIR WITH EACH STEP.

BURST

 SHIMMER AND SPARKLE.

Think for a moment about how you have made people smile. Yes, you can be a clown when you want to.

MOVING CLOUDS

A CLOUD WILL NOT FOLLOW YOU EVERYWHERE.

LEARN HOW TO WHISPER.

Rub some silk across your skin. Luxuriate in this feeling. Purr.

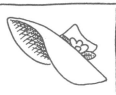

SUN

TINY MIRACLES

THE ELEGANCE OF TOWERING TREES

A SOOTHING SUMMER EVENING BREEZE

HEARING MUSIC EVERYWHERE

A REFRESHING BREATH OF COUNTRY AIR

WRITE AND RECORD YOUR OWN TINY MIRACLES HERE

Think back on the people
you have touched with
your life and who
said they love
you,

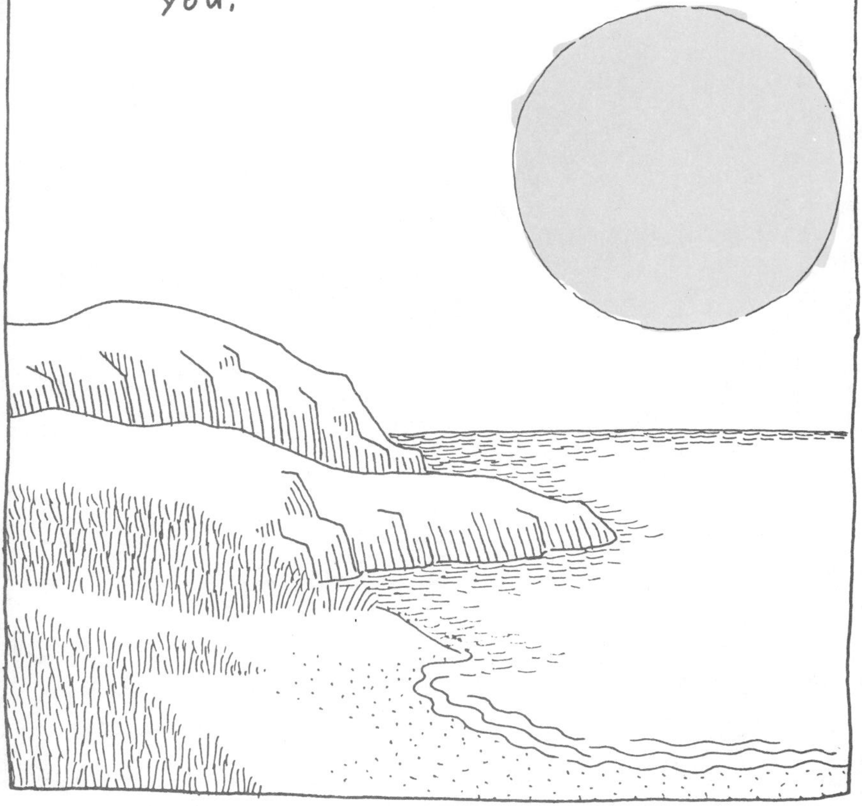

S U N

RAINY DAY PAGE

RAIN WITH ITS ATTENDANT
THUNDER AND LIGHTNING IS
NOISY BUT SOON PASSES.
WITHOUT IT, THOUGH, WE
WOULD HAVE NO FLOWERS
TO SMELL OR
FRUIT TO
SAVOR.
AND MUCH LESS
APPRECIATION
FOR THE SUN.

B U R S T

 WRITE A POEM USING "SUNNY" WORDS.

Buy some beautiful fake flowers and weave a garland to wear on your head. Pretend it's a laurel wreath for all your special achievements.

SUN SPOTS

PLAY HOST TO A BANANA SPLIT PARTY.

Write a letter to someone whom you know will be glad to hear from you. Include a funny picture out of a magazine or a newspaper clipping you think will interest them. Don't forget to place a leaf or a flower or some sparkles in the folded letter before you seal the envelope.

MOVING CLOUDS

PACK YOUR TROUBLES AWAY IN A SAFE PLACE.

 BUILD A SANDCASTLE.

Buy some temporary,
washable tattoos and
decorate your body,
the more outrageous
the better,

SUN

TINY MIRACLES

STARLIGHT AND MOONBEAMS

THE FREEDOM OF DREAMS

THE SPIRIT THAT BACH'S MUSIC HAS

THE DEPTH OF CHARLIE PARKER'S JAZZ

WRITE AND RECORD YOUR OWN TINY MIRACLES HERE

As you jog, pretend that you have just hit the winning home run in the last game of the World Series. You're headed to the dugout where all your teammates will hug you and pour champagne over you. Can't you hear the crowd cheering? Take a bow. You deserve it.

SUN

TINY MIRACLES

A BABY'S CRY

THE QUESTION WHY

A FLOWERED FIELD

A LOVE REVEALED

WRITE AND RECORD YOUR OWN TINY MIRACLES HERE

When your heart seems like it is breaking, write a love song to your dog. Teach her the chorus so you can sing it together. You two make a great duet.

SUN

MOVING CLOUDS

LEARN THE IMPORTANCE OF CALLING YOUR OWN SHOTS.

BURST

SIT QUIETLY AND LISTEN TO A SUNSET.

As the sun sets, watch
the hues of the sky change
from pink to orange to flame
red to a soft yellow green.
Think a moment about who
the greatest Artist really is.

SUN

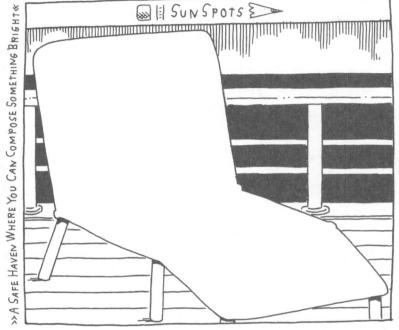

>> A SAFE HAVEN WHERE YOU CAN COMPOSE SOMETHING BRIGHT <<

SUN SPOTS

BURST

THINK BIG, COUNT TO A MILLION.

Remember a song you loved
as a child. Try to recall the
words. If not, then hum it
in your own inimitable voice.

SUN

TINY MIRACLES

INSIDE WARM WHEN OUTSIDE'S COLD

WATCHING WEEKEND DREAMS UNFOLD

FRI

SNIFFING A NEWLY BLOOMED NARCISSUS

READING NOTES FROM THOSE WHO MISS US
xx ♡ xx

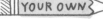

WRITE AND RECORD YOUR OWN TINY MIRACLES HERE

Recite some magical, mysterious incantation to yourself to make the demons disappear. You have banished them from your life. Enjoy!

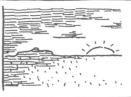

SUN

RAINY DAY PAGE

MAKE THE RAIN CLOUD OVER YOUR HEAD SHOWER YOU WITH FLOWERS...

HOLD OUT YOUR OPEN HANDS SO YOU CAN CATCH THEM.

BURST

RE-READ YOUR FAVORITE CHILDREN'S BOOKS.

Promise yourself
that over the next
few days you'll learn
something new.. a joke,
a magic trick, Then find
an audience to show it off
to. Become the life of
the party and have
a bit of fun, too.

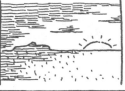

MOVING CLOUDS

LIFE IS A MEAL TO BE ENJOYED TO THE LAST BITE.

BURST

LET A FOUR-YEAR-OLD THROW A SNOWBALL AT YOU.

Draw some stars, cut
them out and stick them
to your ceiling and walls.
Now do some serious
dreaming.

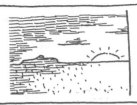

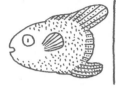

SUN

TINY MIRACLES

THE REALM OF READING BOOKS

THE WAY A GLOWING SUNSET LOOKS

THE SILENCE OF A SNOW FALL

THE SIGHT OF SEEDLINGS GROWING TALL

 WRITE AND RECORD  YOUR OWN  TINY MIRACLES HERE

In the dark of winter,
plant a narcissus bulb in
your kitchen. Nourish it and
watch it grow day by day,
and with it your hope.

SUN

MOVING CLOUDS

TURN YOUR OLD, TIRED WAYS INTO BRIGHT NEW ONES.

BURST

GIVE A BOUQUET OF BALLOONS NEXT TIME.

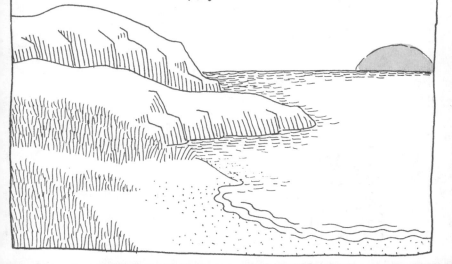

Rummage through
your treasure chest.
Locate a prized possession
and rub it for luck,
If it is an heirloom, then
recall the person who passed
it on to you and how much they
must have valued you. Take
much comfort in your
treasure.

SUNDRIES

CREATE A MAGICAL, PHANTASMAGORICAL STORY AS YOU DREAM. WRITE IT DOWN WHEN YOU WAKE UP.

INCREASE YOUR SMILE PRODUCTION.

Write a letter
to someone you've been
inspired by. Tell
them what they mean
to you.

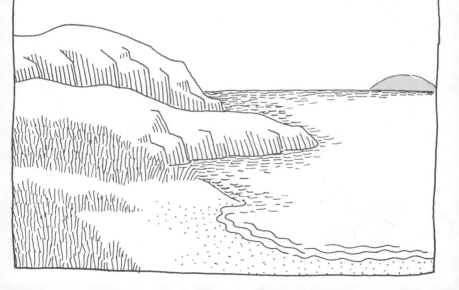

SUN

SunSpots

>> A Safe Haven Where You Can Pen Something Bright <<

BURST

Let Fresh Air Into Your Room, Your Life.

Next time you take a
swim in the bathtub,
bring along your water
paints to decorate the
tile wall with some
pictures. Don't worry,
they will wash off.

SUN

MOVING CLOUDS

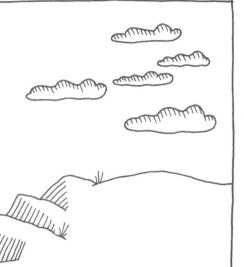

RELAX AT DAY'S END. WAIT FOR TOMORROW'S SUN.

BURST

 WAKE UP HAPPY TOMORROW.

Brew a pot of tea.
Relax and drink a cup.
Notice the leaves at
the bottom? Try to read
them. See what clues
you can decipher to open
up the secrets of your
life. Look only for good
fortune.

SUN

TINY MIRACLES

WATCHING LEAVES TURN FROM GREEN TO GOLD

HEARING THAT THE TRUTH WAS TOLD

A GOOD·MORNING LICK FROM YOUR FAITHFUL PET

THE GOOD THINGS FOR YOU THAT HAVEN'T HAPPENED YET

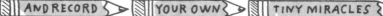
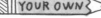

WRITE AND RECORD YOUR OWN TINY MIRACLES HERE

CUT THIS OUT

FILL THIS IN

Dear _____,

Here's a magic word to heal you.

Write back to tell me how it worked!

With love,

S-U-N-L-A-R-G-R-A-M

To

© 1997 · BILL · ZIMMERMAN · PATRICIA · KITCHEN · TOM · BLOOM
"A BOOK OF SUNSHINE" SOURCEBOOKS INC. PUBLISHER

CUT THIS OUT

FILL THIS IN

My good Friend,

I thank my lucky stars that you are part of my world and I'm part of your universe.

Lovingly,

© 1997·BILL·ZIMMERMAN·PATRICIA·KITCHEN·TOM·BLOOM
"A BOOK OF SUNSHINE" SOURCEBOOKS INC. PUBLISHER

SUN-LARGRAM

To

SOMETIMES YOU HAVE TO MAKE YOUR OWN SUNSHINE!

Bill Zimmerman's favorite song as a boy was "You Are My Sunshine"- it never failed to make him smile. So it was inevitable that one day he would write a book of sunshine. A journalist and prize-winning editor, Zimmerman is special projects editor for *Newsday*, one of the nation's largest newspapers. His other books are *A Book of Questions to Keep Thoughts and Feelings*, a new form of diary/journal; *How to Tape Instant Oral Biographies*, a book that teaches you how to capture your family stories on audio and video tape; *Make Beliefs* and *Make Beliefs for Kids*, gift books to spark the imagination; *Lifelines: A Book of Hope*; *The Little Book of Joy*, a book of prayers and meditations, and *DOGMAS: Simple Truths From a Wise Pet*, which holds all the wisdom Zimmerman learned from his dog, Dynamite.

SUNSHINE "
SOMETIMES IT COMES
FROM THE SKY,
SOMETIMES YOU
HAVE TO GENERATE
IT YOURSELF,

Patricia Kitchen is a journalist who specializes in writing about careers and workplace issues. She's always striving to find small solutions to life's big problems. Dreaming up the activities in this little book helped her keep her head above water while she was going through an unhealthy romantic relationship. It also helped her flex her writing muscle, which allowed her to move from being an editor back to being a writer, which she greatly prefers. She now works for *Newsday*.

Tom Bloom maintains a fairly sunny disposition even while working well into the night doing drawings for the New York Times, Newsday, Barron's, Fortune and Games Magazine. He and his family reside where a partly cloudy day can also be a partly sunny day. He subscribes to a number of magazines as well as the notion that most of the shadows in life are caused by standing in our own sunshine.

SHARE WITH US

Dear Reader,

Please share with us the ways you bring sunshine into your own life, as well as some of the "tiny miracles" you have encountered along the way. Perhaps we can incorporate some of them in future editions. We also welcome your comments and suggestions to make *A Book of Sunshine* more useful.

Please write to:

Bill Zimmerman
Guarionex Press
201 West 77 Street
New York, NY 10024